This Book Belongs to

_____

A Children's Treasury of
Mother Goose

Illustrations by

Linda Bleck

STERLING CHILDREN'S BOOKS

New York

I Saw a Ship A-Sailing

I saw a ship a-sailing,
A-sailing on the sea,
And, oh! It was all laden
With pretty things for thee!

There were comfits in the cabin,
And apples in the hold.
The sails were made of silk,
And the masts were made of gold.

The four-and-twenty sailors
That stood between the decks,
Were four-and-twenty white mice
With chains about their necks.

The captain was a duck,
With a packet on his back,
And when the ship began to move,
The captain said, "Quack! Quack!"

The Black Hen

Hickety, pickety, my black hen,
She lays eggs for gentlemen.
Gentlemen come every day,
To see what my black hen doth lay.

The Clever Hen

I had a little hen, the prettiest ever seen.
She washed me the dishes and kept the house clean.
She went to the mill to fetch me some flour,
She brought it home in less than an hour.
She baked me my bread, she brought me my mail,
She sat by the fire and told many a fine tale.

Simple Simon

Simple Simon met a pieman,
Going to the fair.
Said Simple Simon to the pieman,
"Let me taste your ware."

Said the pieman to Simple Simon,
"Show me first your penny."
Said Simple Simon to the pieman,
"Indeed, I have not any."

Simple Simon went a-fishing
For to catch a whale.
All the water he could find
Was in his mother's pail!

Simple Simon went to look
If plums grew on a thistle.
He pricked his fingers very much,
Which made poor Simon whistle.

He went to catch a dicky bird,
And thought he could not fail
Because he had a little salt,
To put upon its tail.

He went for water with a sieve,
But soon it ran all through.
And now poor Simple Simon
Bids you all adieu.

Old Woman, Old Woman

There was an old woman tossed in a basket
Seventeen times as high as the moon.
But where she was going no mortal could tell,
For under her arm she carried a broom.

"Old woman, old woman, old woman," said I,
"Whither, oh whither, oh whither so high?"
"To sweep the cobwebs from the sky,
And I'll be with you by-and-by."

Tweedle-dum and Tweedle-dee

Tweedle-dum and Tweedle-dee
    Resolved to have a battle,
For Tweedle-dum said Tweedle-dee
    Had spoiled his nice new rattle.

Just then flew by a monstrous crow,
    As big as a tar barrel,
Which frightened both the heroes so,
    They quite forgot their quarrel.

Pussy-Cat, Pussy-Cat

"Pussy-cat, pussy-cat,
Where have you been?"
"I've been to London
To visit the Queen."

"Pussy-cat, pussy-cat,
What did you there?"
"I frightened a little mouse
Under the chair."

The Grand Old Duke of York

The grand old Duke of York,
He had ten thousand men.
He marched them up to the top of the hill
And he marched them down again.

And when they were up, they were up,
And when they were down, they were down.
But when they were only halfway up,
They were neither up nor down!

For Want of a Nail

For want of a nail, the shoe was lost,
For want of the shoe, the horse was lost,
For want of the horse, the rider was lost,
For want of the rider, the battle was lost,
For want of the battle, the kingdom was lost,
And all for the want of a horseshoe nail.

Going to St. Ives

As I was going to St. Ives
I met a man with seven wives.
Each wife had seven sacks,
Each sack had seven cats,
Each cat had seven kits.
Kits, cats, sacks, and wives,
How many were going to St. Ives?

The Crooked Sixpence

There was a crooked man, and he went a crooked mile.

He found a crooked sixpence beside a crooked stile.

He bought a crooked cat, which caught a crooked mouse,

And they all lived together in a little crooked house.

Little King Boggen

Little King Boggen,
He built a fine hall.
Pie-crust and pastry-crust,
That was the wall.

The windows were made
Of black puddings and white,
And slated with pancakes—
You ne'er saw the like!

The Lion and the Unicorn

The lion and the unicorn were fighting for the crown.
The lion beat the unicorn all around the town.
Some gave them white bread, and some gave them brown,
Some gave them plum-cake and sent them out of town.

The Ten O'Clock Scholar

A diller, a dollar, a ten o'clock scholar!
What makes you come so soon?
You used to come at ten o'clock,
But now you come at noon.

The Little Girl with a Curl

There was a little girl,
Who had a little curl,
Right in the middle of her forehead.
When she was good,
She was very, very good.
But when she was bad she was horrid.

To Market

To market, to market, to buy a fat pig,
Home again, home again, jiggety jig.
To market, to market, to buy a fat hog,
Home again, home again, jiggety jog.

To market, to market, to buy a plum bun,
Home again, home again, market is done.

I Had a Little Husband

I had a little husband,
No bigger than my thumb,
I put him in a pint pot,
And there I bid him drum.
I bought a little handkerchief
To wipe his little nose,
And a pair of little garters
To tie his little hose.

The Flying Pig

Dickory, dickory, dare,
The pig flew up in the air.
The man in brown soon brought him down,
Dickory, dickory, dare.

Jack Jelf

Little Jack Jelf
Was put on the shelf
Because he could not spell "pie."
When his aunt, Mrs. Grace,
Saw his sorrowful face,
She could not help saying, "Oh, fie!"

And since Master Jelf
Was put on the shelf
Because he could not spell "pie,"
Let him stand there so grim,
And no more about him,
For I wish him a very good-bye!

Wee Willie Winkie

Wee Willie Winkie runs through the town,
Upstairs and downstairs, in his nightgown,
Rapping at the window,
Crying through the lock,
"Are the children in their beds?
It's past eight o'clock!"

For my mom, Virginia
— L.B.

STERLING CHILDREN'S BOOKS
New York

An Imprint of Sterling Publishing
1166 Avenue of the Americas
New York, NY 10036

Illustrations © 2009 by Linda Bleck
Paperback edition published in 2015.
Previously published by Sterling Publishing, Co., Inc. in a different format in 2009.

Designed by Josh Simons, Simonsays Design!

ISBN 978-1-4549-1473-0

Distributed in Canada by Sterling Publishing
c/o Canadian Manda Group, 664 Annette Street
Toronto, Ontario, Canada M6S 2C8
Distributed in the United Kingdom by GMC Distribution Services
Castle Place, 166 High Street, Lewes, East Sussex, England BN7 1XU
Distributed in Australia by Capricorn Link (Australia) Pty. Ltd.
P.O. Box 704, Windsor, NSW 2756, Australia

For information about custom editions, special sales, and premium and corporate purchases,
please contact Sterling Special Sales at 800-805-5489 or specialsales@sterlingpublishing.com.

Manufactured in China
Lot #:
2 4 6 8 10 9 7 5 3 1
01/15

www.sterlingpublishing.com/kids